Beyond the Park Loop Road

Continuing the exploration of Acadia National Park

To Linda, my wife, friend, and inspiration; she has been my partner in discovering the beauty of Acadia National Park and Mount Desert Island.

Beyond the Park Loop Road

Continuing the exploration of Acadia National Park

Written and Photographed by Robert A. Thayer

Down East Books Camden, Maine

ISBN 0-89272-522-2

Designed by Lindy Gifford

Cover photograph: *Bass Harbor Marsh offers both beauty and tranquillity.*
Title page photograph: *Surf pounds the rocks at Seawall.*

1   3   5   4   2

Printed in China

Down East Books
P.O. Box 679
Camden, ME 04843
BOOK ORDERS: 1-800-685-7962

Library of Congress Card Number: 00-111159

Contents

The sun rises over Somes Pond.

Acknowledgments

I would like to thank the following people who contributed their time and expertise in making this book more than it would have been.

Joan Furnari, Bryant Woods, Tom Vining, and Linda Thayer, who read the text, made corrections, and gave invaluable editorial direction.

Mike Furnari, Robert Pyle, Henry Raup, Phoebe Milliken, and Hugh Dwelley for sharing their knowledge and stories of the area and for confirming dates and other factual information.

Brook Childrey curator of Acadia National Park's historic collection, and Jaylene Roths, curator of the Mount Desert Island Historical Society for their assistance in finding historic photographs.

Sarah F. Desbiens of the Historic American Engineering Record for the use of that publication's artwork.

Editor Chris Cornell and designer Lindy Gifford for organizing my photographs and words into a book. And all the people at Down East Books—particularly Alice Devine—who helped me in many ways.

West Pond Cove at Schoodic.

Beyond the road, beyond the beach, beyond the crowded summit peaks, another side of Acadia National Park waits to be discovered. It is this other Acadia that draws returning visitors, year after year. They come back to hike one more trail, to climb one more mountain, to discover one more hidden cove in the seemingly endless diversity of Mount Desert Island. To those who have felt this tug, Acadia is more than a national park, it is a state of mind. This book is for those whose spirit takes them beyond the Park Loop Road in their exploration of this special place.

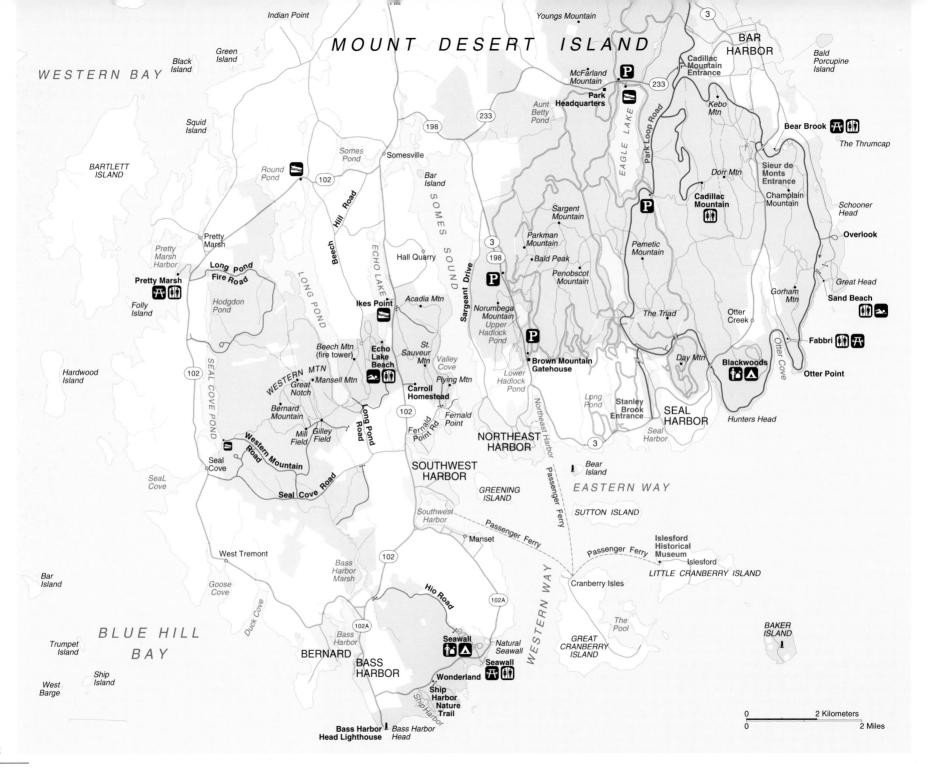

MOUNT DESERT ISLAND

WESTERN BAY

Indian Point

Youngs Mountain

BAR HARBOR

Black Island

Green Island

Bald Porcupine Island

③

Cadillac Mountain Entrance

McFarland Mountain

P

Park Headquarters

233

Kebo Mtn

Bear Brook 🏕🚻

The Thrumcap

Squid Island

BARTLETT ISLAND

198

233

Aunt Betty Pond

Dorr Mtn

Sieur de Monts Entrance

Somes Pond

Somesville

P

Cadillac Mountain 🚻

Champlain Mountain

Round Pond 📷

102

Bar Island

Eagle Lake

Park Loop Road

Schooner Head

Pretty Marsh

Pretty Marsh Harbor

Pretty Marsh 🚻🏕

Folly Island

Hodgdon Pond

Beech Hill Road

Hall Quarry

Sargent Mountain

Parkman Mountain

Bald Peak

Pemetic Mountain

P

198

③

ECHO LAKE

Long Pond Fire Road

LONG POND

SOMES SOUND

Acadia Mtn

P

Norumbega Mountain

Upper Hadlock Pond

Penobscot Mountain

Overlook

Gorham Mtn

Sand Beach 🚻🏊

Ikes Point 📷

SEAL COVE POND

Hardwood Island

102

WESTERN MTN

Great Notch

Beech Mtn (fire tower)

Echo Lake Beach 🏊🚻

St. Sauveur Mtn

Valley Cove

Brown Mountain Gatehouse

P

The Triad

Lower Hadlock Pond

Day Mtn

Otter Creek

Fabbri 🚻🏕

Blackwoods 🚻🏕

Otter Cove

Otter Point

Mansell Mtn

Carroll Homestead

Flying Mtn

Fernald Point

Bernard Mountain

Mill Field

Gilley Field

Long Pond Road

102

Fernald Point Rd

NORTHEAST HARBOR

Northeast Harbor

Long Pond

Stanley Brook Entrance

SEAL HARBOR

Seal Harbor

Hunters Head

③

Seal Cove

SeaL Cove

Western Mountain Road

Seal Cove Road

SOUTHWEST HARBOR

Bear Island

EASTERN WAY

Trumpet Island

West Barge

Ship Island

Goose Cove

Duck Cove

West Tremont

Bass Harbor Marsh

102

GREENING ISLAND

Passenger Ferry

SUTTON ISLAND

Southwest Harbor

Passenger Ferry

Manset

Passenger Ferry

Islesford Historical Museum

Islesford

LITTLE CRANBERRY ISLAND

Bar Island

102A

Bass Harbor

Hio Road

102A

Cranberry Isles

WESTERN WAY

The Pool

BAKER ISLAND

Ship Island

BERNARD

BASS HARBOR

102A

Seawall 🚻🏕

Natural Seawall

Seawall 🏕🚻

Wonderland

Ship Harbor Nature Trail

GREAT CRANBERRY ISLAND

GREAT CRANBERRY ISLAND

BLUE HILL BAY

Bass Harbor Head Lighthouse

Bass Harbor Head

Ship Harbor

0		2 Kilometers
0		2 Miles

Getting Started

To appreciate all that Acadia National Park encompasses, one must first understand the geography of the surrounding area. Acadia is situated almost entirely on the third largest island on the East Coast. Roughly a circle measuring twenty miles in diameter, Mount Desert Island is bisected by Somes Sound, an arm of the Atlantic Ocean. A range of mountains runs across the island from east to west, and these peaks are separated by glacially carved valleys, many of which are filled by freshwater lakes.

The shoreline is rugged and rocky, having emerged only twelve to fifteen thousand years ago from beneath a retreating continental glacier. Time and erosion have yet to wear the coast into gentle, sandy beaches. Although the shaping of the island is a recent geologic occurrence, the formation of the rocks themselves took place nearly four hundred million years ago. Deep within the Earth, colliding continents generated large masses of molten rock that pushed their way into the overlying bedrock. When this upward movement stopped, the magma slowly cooled and became granite. Erosion has since exposed these rounded mounds of rock, which are now the mountains of Acadia.

Mount Desert Island is situated on the border of two great forest communities. To the north are the pure stands of conifers, while to the south are the rich, broad-leaved deciduous trees. The vegetation of the island is a sampling from both of these communities: spruce, fir, and hemlock, as well as oak, aspen, and beech. Each fall, this diversity is dramatically displayed as the reds and yellows of the deciduous trees glow against a backdrop of dark evergreens.

The surrounding ocean is a major player in the climate of the island and in determining which plants and animals make their homes here. This great body of water absorbs heat in the summer and releases it in the winter, moderating the seasons on Mount Desert Island. Acadian winters

The surf continues to define Acadia's shoreline.

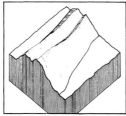

1. *Mountain Formation*

2. *Glacial Erosion*

3. *Present Landscape*

JOE KORZENIEWSKI

can be cold, but offshore breezes often turn snow to rain. Spring arrives early here, with a flurry of blossoms and bugs that may linger into June. Summers are warm and dry, but the sea conditions the air so that July and August temperatures along the coast are nearly always cooler than those just a few miles inland.

Geology and climate have conspired to produce an environment where all life can find sustenance and comfort. From its earliest human history, Mount Desert has proven to be unique and highly desirable. Native Americans, European explorers, early American settlers, and modern-day visitors have all come seeking the treasures of this island. Here the forces of Nature have combined with human history to create a place that only a national park such as Acadia could preserve. Yet many visitors confine their experience to driving the Park Loop Road, which—although beautiful—presents only one facet of the park.

The journey to the "other Acadia" begins upon leaving the summit of Cadillac Mountain and the Park Loop Road.

Fall colors like these at Beech Mountain on Long Pond vividly display the diversity of plants in the park.

Seasons bring dramatic changes to the Acadian landscape at Somes Sound.

Geology and climate conspire to create an environment of abundance and beauty off the Schoodic Peninsula.

THE EASTERN LOOP

Travel west on Route 233 toward the center of the island. At the end of Route 233, take a left onto Route 198, and head toward Northeast Harbor. After traveling just over a mile, follow the road that diverges to the right.

Sargeant Drive parallels the eastern shore of Somes Sound.

Sargeant Drive

This is a narrow, winding route; restricted to automobiles only, it follows the eastern shore of Somes Sound. Considered the only true fjord on the east coast of the United States, the sound is a product of glacial action. Twenty thousand years ago, the entire area was covered with nearly a mile of ice. This moving glacier scoured the bed of an existing stream, turned it into a steep U-shaped valley, and deposited debris at what is now the mouth of the sound, called the "narrows." As the glacier melted and the ocean level rose, the valley was flooded. Although it's not noticeable from the shoreline today, the walls of the sound plunge another one hundred fifty feet to the valley's floor. This fact is not lost on the lobstermen who ply these waters. Even the buoys close to shore may be attached to traps that are sixty to ninety feet below the surface.

With the incoming tide, sea level in the sound rises, and with this rush of water come schools of herring and other fish, following their planktonic food supply. In turn, these small forage species attract harbor porpoises that can often be seen patrolling Somes Sound. Ospreys and bald eagles, perched on shoreline treetops, also look for fish in the rich and gentle waters. Although each tide partially renews the water in the sound, dozens of tidal cycles are required to bring about a complete exchange. This makes the sound more vulnerable to pollution, underscoring the importance of limits on the type and scope of development along its shores.

The mountains across the water from Sargeant Drive are, from right to left, Acadia, the highest peak, with the flat top; Saint Sauveur, with its dramatic vertical cliff face; and Flying Mountain. According to Indian legend, this last peak was once the top of Acadia Mountain, but it flew off and landed in the sound.

The waters of the sound are deep and rich in marine life.

At the mouth of Somes Sound, on the western shore, is an open, grassy hillside called Fernald Point. One of the first French settlements in New England (New France) was established at this site in 1613. Led by Father Pierre Biard, a party of sixteen Jesuit priests and fifty settlers set sail from France aboard the *Jonas* and headed for Kadisquit (now Bangor), a site that had been visited by the explorer Samuel de Champlain. As they approached the coast, a thick fog set in, and the vessel took refuge in a protected harbor. When the fog lifted two days later, the Frenchmen found themselves off Mount Desert Island. Led to Fernald Point by native Abnakis, the Jesuits found it to their liking and immediately established their mission, naming it Saint Sauveur.

The newcomers had barely begun planting crops, building a fort, and baptizing the natives when their settlement was discovered by the English. Sir Samuel Argall from the Virginia Colony, patrolling the coast on the *Treasurer*, destroyed the mission, killing three Frenchmen. The survivors were taken to Virginia and later released. This was likely one of the first confrontations in the French and Indian Wars.

Animosity between the French and the English kept the coast of Maine, including Mount Desert Island, inhospitable to settlers from both countries for nearly a hundred and fifty years. However, when in 1759 the English triumphed over the French in Quebec, marking the end of the French and Indian Wars, coastal Maine was finally open for settlement.

Sargeant Drive ends in the town of Northeast Harbor. The town bustles with activity in the summer as the harbor fills with boats of every size and shape, from all corners of the world.

Somes Sound allows the ocean to penetrate five miles into the center of Mount Desert Island.

The Brown Mountain Gatehouse

After leaving Northeast Harbor, follow Route 198 north. At the top of the first hill, you will notice a large stone house on your right. Just beyond is a parking lot.

Built in 1932 by John D. Rockefeller Jr., this beautiful structure is the companion to the Jordan Pond Gatehouse in Seal Harbor. Both were intended as residences for gatekeepers who would control access to Acadia's carriage road system. They were deeded to the National Park Service shortly after completion and became housing for park employees, as they remain to this day.

Brown Mountain Gatehouse was designed by Grosvenor Atterbury in the late Tudor Revival style. Made of locally quarried granite, plus red brick and cypress, the complex is laid out in a half-hexagonal design. Two towers frame the massive cypress gates, which open onto the carriage road system and are connected to the "lodge" by an impressive wall of stone.

Visitors may notice that although this building was named for a mountain, there is no Brown Mountain in the park. Indeed, Acadia features many place names that date back to an earlier time. Prior to 1860, few mountains were named on official maps. With the coming of summer visitors between 1860 and 1870, however, nearly all the local peaks were given names. When the national park was established, many of these were changed.

George B. Dorr, one of Acadia's founding fathers and the park's first superintendent, systematically

The Brown Mountain Gatehouse reflects the Tudor Revival style.

SARAH F. DESBIENS

Upper Hadlock Pond is crowned by Parkman Mountain, in the distance.

changed place names to reflect local conditions, native Indian custom, or the French heritage of Mount Desert Island. (To be precise, Dorr requested the changes; the U.S. Board on Geographic Names had to approve them.) This may lead to confusion as some of the old monikers continue to be used by local residents. Brown Mountain is a good example. The peak, across the street from the gatehouse, was originally named for John Brown, who owned acreage just north of the mountain. But in 1918, its name was changed to Norumbega, after the fabled city of gold sought by early explorers.

Across the street from the Brown Mountain Gatehouse is a small, unpaved road that leads to the edge of Lower Hadlock Pond. In the late 1880s the frozen waters of this pond were a source of income for Captain Horace Roberts of Northeast Harbor. His crews cut one-hundred pound blocks of ice, hauled them to the top of a small knoll south of the pond, then let gravity take them down a wooden sluice to an icehouse near the harbor. There the blocks were loaded onto schooners and taken to cities like Boston, New York, Philadelphia, and Baltimore, where they helped preserve food in the finest households.

Continuing along Route 198 beyond the Brown Mountain Gatehouse, you will come to a small body of water on the right. This is Upper Hadlock Pond, and in the distance is Parkman Mountain. A parking lot at the top of the next hill allows access to the carriage roads and to the trails that lead up Parkman Mountain and Sargent Mountain. (Note that the spelling of Sargent Mountain is not the same as Sargeant Drive. According to Robert Pyle, Northeast Harbor librarian, the road was named for Samuel Duncan Sargeant, a prominent summer resident who had it built, while the mountain was named for a year-round family that owned land in the area.)

15

THE WESTERN LOOP

Often referred to as the "quiet side," the western half of Mount Desert Island offers opportunities that are often missed in the rush and traffic of the eastern half.

Follow route 198 in a northerly direction until you come to a traffic light and the junction with route 102. At the light take a left, and drive slowly through Somesville, taking in its quaint beauty.

Somesville was the economic center of Mount Desert Island in the mid-1800s.

Dawn breaks on Somes Harbor.

Somesville

This small village is the gateway to the island's quiet side, and visiting it is a step back in time. In 1761, Abraham Somes of Gloucester, Massachusetts, built a small log cabin in a quiet, sheltered harbor at the head of the sound. Noting that the area's large oaks would provide lumber and its streams would furnish hydropower, Somes determined that this site could best provide the resources for an eventual community. The following year, he returned with his wife and four children to establish the first permanent settlement on Mount Desert Island. He called it "Betwixt the Hills," referring to the two mountains, Norumbega and Acadia, between which he had passed as he sailed up the sound. As poetic as the name may strike us today, Somes was apparently less concerned with the beauty and uniqueness of the area than with the feasibility of surviving on this wild, unsettled island.

As his family grew (to thirteen children) and other families came to settle in the village, Somesville began to prosper. By 1836, it had become the economic center of the island. Eben Hamor of Town Hill recorded, "one small store, one blacksmith shop, one shoemaker's shop, one

Two kayakers explore the shores of Somes Harbor.

A wooden footbridge spans the Mill Pond in Somesville.

tan-yard, two shipyards, one bark mill, one saw mill, one lath mill, one shingle mill, one grist mill, and one schoolhouse."

In 1855, Charles Tracy, a New York lawyer and the father-in-law of banker J. P. Morgan, assembled a party of twenty-six friends and relatives who traveled three days from New York to spend a month in Somesville. Once settled, they explored the island by foot and horse-drawn wagon. Their adventure is recorded in the "Tracy Log Book" and in the artwork of Frederic Church, who was among the party. The power of Church's paintings and those of others who made similar treks to the area brought the unique beauty of Mount Desert to the city dwellers of Boston, New York, and Philadelphia. Thus began a new era in the history of the island. From that day through the present, local residents have opened their doors to those seeking a quiet moment with Nature.

Today, although the mills of Somesville are gone, the houses and the character of this small coastal village remain as they were a hundred years ago, when life was slower and neighbors were more than just the people who lived next door.

Beech Mountain

At the blinking light just south of Somesville, turn right onto the Pretty Marsh Road, then make a left at the next intersection, onto Beech Hill Road. Continue until the pavement ends in a small parking lot.

Across from the parking area, a short trail leads to Beech Cliff, a sheer rock face rising from the shore of Echo Lake. This outcropping overlooks the narrow valley and provides an impressive vista. At the southern end of Echo Lake is a manmade beach, one of the few public, freshwater beaches on Mount Desert Island. You can reach it from the cliff via a steep and difficult descent, but it is more easily accessed by vehicle from Route 102.

At the southern end of the Beech Mountain parking lot is a flat, wooded trail that was once part of the road from Somesville to Southwest Harbor. Abandoned after the construction of Route 102, it has now been reclaimed by the forest. At the end of the old road, the path forks. To the left,

The fire tower on the summit of Beech Mountain is visible from Beech Cliff.

The view from Beech Cliff is worth the short walk from the parking lot.

the Canada Cliffs Trail loops back to the parking lot via Beech Cliff. To the right is the Valley Trail, which eventually connects with the South Ridge Trail leading to the summit of Beech Mountain.

Whether you climb as far as the top of the mountain or not, this trail is worthy of a visit in its own right. Towering trees and large, fern-covered boulders create the impression that you have become a creature in a terrarium. A close inspection of the vegetation reveals a myriad of lichens, mosses, and ferns. Although visitors may feel dwarfed by the surroundings, the world of the small dominates here. The sense of mystery along the Valley Trail is heightened when fog shrouds the distant view and forces your eyes to the lush green world that surrounds the trail.

Reindeer lichens and bunchberry dogwood

Field Horsetail (Equisetum arvense)

Hikers stop to appreciate the scene along the Valley Trail.

19

Viewed from the back side of Beech Mountain, Long Pond and the western horizon are a beautiful sight.

The waters of Man O' War Brook plunge dramatically into Somes Sound.

Like most of Acadia's peaks, Beech Mountain has an open summit with panoramic views of the other mountains to the east and of the ocean and islands to the south. At the top is a fire tower, which—when it is manned and accessible—increases the view to a full 360 degrees.

When you are ready for new sights, return to Route 102; take a right at the blinking light, and head toward Southwest Harbor. Three miles from Somesville, on the right, is the parking area for Acadia Mountain. Just to the north and across the street from the parking area, a fire road leads to the waters of Somes Sound. Closed to vehicles, the trail traverses the valley between Acadia and Saint Sauveur Mountains, and parallels Man O' War Brook, which empties into Somes Sound over a small waterfall. Like most of those in the park, the Man O' War Brook cataract is active only when winter snows melt in early spring or after a particularly heavy rain. This waterfall once provided sailing vessels with a rare opportunity to replenish their water supply without going ashore. Because of the steep walls of the valley, British warships could maneuver close enough to place a sluice-board into the falls and fill their barrels. In 1878, the Russian naval vessel S.S. *Cimbria* was the last recorded vessel to use the falls in such a way. (Today, drinking from any unfiltered freshwater source is not recommended, primarily because of the protozoan known as giardia.)

The Carroll Homestead

About a mile and a half south of the Acadia Mountain trailhead, a dirt road on the left leads to the Carroll Homestead.

In 1820, John Carroll, an Irish immigrant, arrived in Southwest Harbor to work temporarily as a woodsman. There he met Rachel Lurvey, who cared for him after a logging accident. The two fell in love and were married in 1822. Three years later they built a small house on an un-claimed parcel of land at the foot of Dog (now Saint Sauveur) Mountain. For the next ninety-two years, John, Rachel, and their descendants would live, prosper, and raise their families in this "Mountain House." Though they were squatters on the land, it eventually became theirs by law.

In his book, *Four Generations In Maine,* Henry Raup chronicles the details of the Carrolls' life and, in so doing, documents the struggles of the early Maine settlers who made their living off the land. In 1917 the Carroll Homestead was vacated as a permanent residence but was maintained for family gatherings and special events. In 1982 it was donated to Acadia National Park, where it will remain as an example of the subsistence farms that were so important to the settling of Mount Desert Island and will live on as a lasting memorial to the Carroll Family.

John and Rachel Carroll raised a big family in their "Mountain House."

The homestead was occupied by Carrolls until 1917.

The Carroll Homestead is a reminder of the subsistance farmers who settled early New England.

Valley Cove is a small, protected harbor cut into the shore of Somes Sound.

Valley Cove

Continue south toward Southwest Harbor on Route 102, and in a short distance from the Carroll Homestead, take a left onto Fernald Point Road. In less than a mile, Fernald Cove will be on your right and just beyond that, you'll find a small parking lot on the left. The trail that starts here was once a road and now provides a flat, easy walk to Valley Cove and Somes Sound.

Nestled between Saint Sauveur and Flying Mountains is the small but deep harbor of Valley Cove. Cruising sailboats often anchor here as it is protected from the swells of the open ocean and from all but northerly winds. The cliff face on the side of Saint Sauveur is a historic nesting area for peregrine falcons, which were reintroduced to the park and may again find this mountain to their liking.

Stretching up the side of this cliff is a talus slope, created as the glaciers and subsequent erosion pulled stones from the mountainside and piled them at its base. A trail traverses the rocky slope and continues into the wooded shoreline, heading toward Man O' War Brook. From this area, other paths lead to the summits of Saint Sauveur and Flying Mountains, which both provide views of the sound and Southwest Harbor. Those not wishing to hike or climb may simply find a relaxing spot on the shore and appreciate the pageant of sailing vessels plying the waters of Somes Sound.

Seawall

Return to Route 102 and take a left toward Southwest Harbor. After passing through the town, turn left onto Route 102A toward the village of Manset and Seawall Campground. After about three miles, you will come to the ocean, where the road snakes across a narrow stretch of storm beach, or seawall. Parking is limited at this spot, but just a few hundred yards beyond are the Seawall Picnic Area and Campground, where you can leave your vehicle and explore the rocky beach.

When nor'easters blow into the Gulf of Maine, which is common, the shore here gets pounded by strong winds and high surf. At such times, the sea picks up hundreds of rounded cobblestones the size of bowling balls and tosses them fifty feet onto the road. Plows are sometimes needed to clear the pavement. It is just this phenomenon that created the seawall and others like it along this exposed shoreline.

The beaches in the area offer samples of the rock types found on Mount Desert Island and even on the mainland. Deposited here as the glaciers retreated, these stones have been worked by the sea into smooth, rounded cobbles. Along the shoreline are several outcroppings of gray, speckled bedrock called the Cranberry Island series (named for the place where it was first identified). Although static in appearance today, this area was the site of a dramatic geologic event four hundred millions years ago. Blasted from a volcano that has long since weathered away, hot ash and molten rock settled and cooled into the igneous outcroppings that now mark the beach.

The Seawall is just that: a barrier of stone built by the surf.

The sea expends its energy on the shore at Seawall.

The cobble beach at Wonderland is a vivid example of the sea's ability to sculpt and arrange rocks.

Wonderland

About a mile beyond the Seawall picnic area is a small parking lot on the left. A flat, half-mile trail leads to the ocean.

This is the area of Acadia known as Wonderland, where the trail's end loops around a small peninsula, displaying three distinct shoreline environments. A short scramble to the right leads to a small, unnamed cove and a spectacular cobble beach. The same forces that created Seawall are also at work here. Gravity and the action of the water have arranged the stones by size, ranging from large to small as you get closer to the ocean. Listen to the surf as it continues the process of rounding, smoothing, and rearranging the cobbles.

The headland at the end of the peninsula is exposed to the full force of the ocean. Great, flat slabs of granite gradually step into the intertidal zone and the sea beyond. This is the perfect spot to lie back, listen to the surf, and watch a parade of sailboats pass before you.

The east side of the peninsula features a shallow, protected cove. Offshore ledges shelter the shoreline from heavy surf, and when the tide is right the cove becomes ideal feeding grounds for shorebirds and gulls. Watch, too, for the bald eagles that often perch on Long Ledge; this small, sandy island just beyond the peninsula is exposed at low tide.

Eider ducks can often be seen in the waters near Wonderland, for Mount Desert Island is the southern edge of the common eider's breeding range. In the summer months, rafts of brown females and young congregate in large numbers, seeking food in the rich shallow waters off the rocky coast. They reach the mussels, clams, sea

Low tide exposes the barnacles that cover the rocks at Long Ledge.

Wonderland offers an extensive intertidal zone.

The Rugosa Rose has found a home along Acadia's rocky, often foggy shores.

urchins, sea stars, and crabs that form their diet by diving to depths of up to sixty feet, just outside the breaking waves. Their catch is swallowed whole and crushed in a large gizzard. After feeding for twenty to thirty minutes, they will move offshore en masse to preen and digest their meal.

The Rugosa Rose, a nonnative plant, has found a home on the shores of Mount Desert Island, and nowhere is this more evident than at Wonderland. Here the hardy plant flourishes with its roots in the poor, rocky soil and its deep green leaves in the salty air. In summer its blossoms add red highlights to the pink and gray granite shoreline, and their sweet aroma combines with that of balsam and spruce. As fall approaches the bushes are heavy with large, red rose hips that look and taste like small crabapples. Often used to make tea, these hips are said to be high in Vitamin C.

25

Ship Harbor

A short distance from the Wonderland parking area is the Ship Harbor Nature Trail. A one-and-a-half-mile (round trip) route over varied terrain leads from the forest to a saltwater marsh and, finally, to the open, rocky shore. Although the trail is rated easy, the terrain can be rugged, so good footgear is recommended.

The story of Ship Harbor's name goes back to the War of Independence, when a Yankee privateer, running from a British man-of-war, sailed into the narrow mouth of this small harbor at high tide. The crew escaped into the woods, but the vessel ran so hard aground that even subsequent high tides did not set her free. The privateer eventually broke apart, but legend has it that for years her timbers could be seen in the waters of what became known as Ship Harbor.

A fine nature trail winds along the edge of the protected anchorage and eventually ends at a rocky outcropping overlooking the ocean. These granite headlands allow easy access to a variety of tide pools, each providing a window into one of Acadia's most unusual habitats.

The pools in the upper intertidal zone are recharged only by the very highest tides. Left undisturbed for days or even weeks, the seawater trapped here is heated and evaporated by the blazing sun, increasing its salinity. Rain may help to control the temperature, but it also dilutes the pools with fresh water. These extremes limit the type of organisms that can make this zone their home. One such plant, *Enteromorpha intestinalis*, is a long, thin, green algae. The hollow cavity in each strand traps oxygen bubbles produced during photosynthesis, causing it to rise to the surface where, as its name implies, the plant looks like a mass of green intestines..

The pools closest to the shore are refreshed with each new tide, providing a more hospitable habitat for a greater number of organisms. Encrusted with pink coralline algae and little forests of purple weeds, these tide pools present a colorful display of miniature marine life. Red, green, and brown seaweeds provide food and shelter for periwinkles, shrimp, and barnacles that thrive in this seawater environment. Small, conical-shelled limpets *(Acmaea testudinalis)* slowly roam the tide pools, eating microscopic vegetation with their rasping mouth parts. Limpets are close relatives of periwinkles and other single-shelled mollusks, but the edges of their nearly symmetrical shells precisely fit the contours of the small granite plots that they call home. This feature allows them to attach themselves to the rock, thereby protecting them from high surf and hungry predators.

Rarely are large organisms found in these upper pools, though the occasional sea star or urchin may find itself trapped as the water retreats. Hermit crabs and little green crabs are likewise only temporary guests.

The Ship Harbor Nature Trail is laid out in a nearly perfect figure eight. If you followed the harbor on the way out, you might want to take the wooded trail back to the parking area. The first section rises over a rocky knoll where the soil is poorly developed and inadequate for large trees. Here the exposed granite is covered with lichens and mosses, which are beginning the process of soil formation. Once a small amount of earth is

Ship Harbor is often shrouded in fog.

26

produced, blueberries, huckleberries, and bayberries flourish in this open, sunlit habitat. Eventually eastern larch and red spruce trees take hold and continue the succession of vegetation that eventually leads to a mature evergreen forest. As the trail approaches the center of the figure eight, the soil is richer and the forest more developed. In this cool, dark hollow the dead branches of the spruce trees are draped with beard lichen, and the trunks of many trees are swollen with massive burls, giving the forest an ominous and surreal appearance. For such a short trail, Ship Harbor beautifully spans the variety of terrain—from exposed, rocky shoreline to dense, evergreen woodland—that is the hallmark of the Acadian coast.

Enteromorpha, *or Hollow Green Seaweed*

Crumb of Bread sponge and periwinkles

Limpet on an algae-encrusted rock

The quiet water found in tide pools is host to a plethora of marine life.

Hermit crab

27

Bass Harbor Head Light

Less than a mile south of Ship Harbor, the road takes a sharp turn to the right into Bass Harbor. Turn left at this intersection, and proceed to the Bass Harbor Head Lighthouse. A short, paved walkway leads down to the light itself, but to experience the classic view of it you will need to descend a set of steep wooden stairs to a cleared platform on the rocky shore below the parking area.

Built in 1858 of stone and brick, this lighthouse marks the entrance to Bass Harbor and Blue Hill Bay. The light was automated in 1974 and is still maintained by the Coast Guard, although the surrounding land is part of Acadia National Park. This is the only lighthouse on Mount Desert Island, so it is one of the most photographed structures in Acadia.

The path leading to the viewpoint is surrounded by a nearly pure stand of white spruce, one of the most extensive such forest communities on the coast of Maine. Also known as cat spruce because of its pungent odor, this tree can be identified by its plump, light blue needles, which tend to curl upward from the branches. More commonly thought of as a Canadian tree, the white spruce seems to thrive on the salty, windswept

The same lighthouse has been guarding Bass Harbor since 1858.

White spruce

shores along the down east coast.

Upon leaving the lighthouse and passing through the small town of Bass Harbor, the road forks. The route to the right leads back to Southwest Harbor and is the most direct way to reach the center of the island. The road to the left winds along the back side of the island, past the towns of Bernard, West Tremont, and Pretty Marsh.

The Pretty Marsh Picnic Area was built in the late 1930s and early 1940s by the Civilian Conservation Corps, which completed many other projects in the park. Normally a picnic area would not be included in a photographic guidebook like this, but the one at Pretty Marsh is much more than a place to eat. Because of its limited parking and an out-of-the-way location, few visitors include this stop in their itinerary. When you enter this part of the park, you will quickly sense a difference.

The mature evergreen forest creates a dark canopy. Even on hot summer days this area may be ten degrees cooler than the rest of the island. At the bottom of a rather steep, wooded hillside is a covered picnic site and a stairway to the shore below. The surf is rarely rough in this protected location, but the cold ocean water often creates fog and a feeling of mystery in the quiet harbor.

Early light filters through the trees at Pretty Marsh.

The sun sets at Pretty Marsh.

BEYOND MOUNT DESERT ISLAND

If Acadia is more than the Park Loop Road, it is also more than Mount Desert Island. Special circumstances have led to the park boundary's being extended beyond MDI. These areas include parts of the Cranberry Isles, Schoodic Peninsula, and Isle au Haut.

Bear Island Light was built in 1839 and only decommissioned in 1981.

This osprey, a seasonal resident of Sutton Island, has an impressive view of the harbor.

The Cranberry Isles

Though they are separate and distinct in many ways, The Cranberry Isles collectively comprise a single town encompassing five islands: Bear, Sutton, Baker, Little Cranberry, and Great Cranberry. They can be reached only by boat, and access is limited at Bear and Sutton Islands, as they are inhabited exclusively by summer residents. Little Cranberry and Great Cranberry each have about one hundred year-round residents. Their populations triple in the summer, when seasonal residents arrive. Baker Island is uninhabited and is part of Acadia National Park. The mail boat from North-east Harbor makes stops at Sutton, Little Cranberry, and Great Cranberry several times each day in the summer and less frequently in the off-season. Passenger space is available but limited. Two privately owned boats offer nature tours to Baker Island and Little Cranberry during the summer months. Consult park publications or the Visitors Center for information about these trips.

Though the islands were originally named for their cranberry bogs, there is no longer any active cranberry harvesting here. In 1928 the bogs were drained for mosquito control.

Bear Island Light

Situated just outside Northeast Harbor, Bear Island provides a commanding view of the surrounding area and, so, was the logical location for a lighthouse. Its name apparently reflects the barren nature of the island's western half ("bear" and "bare" were often used interchangeably in early nomenclature). Built in 1839, the light provided a beacon for every vessel entering the harbor, from large, cargo-carrying schooners to small lobster-boats. Decommissioned by the U.S. Coast Guard in 1981, when it was replaced by an offshore buoy, the Bear Island tower was one of the last manned lighthouses on the coast of Maine. Today it is owned by the National Park Service and is leased to an individual for residential use. The light still burns, however, and remains a landmark for all those who sail this busy thoroughfare.

Bear Island Light leads pleasure boats and commercial vessels alike into Northeast Harbor.

Islesford is still very much a working harbor.

Islesford

Islesford is the village on Little Cranberry Island. Unlike the yachts and pleasure boats in Northeast Harbor, the vessels here are mostly used for commercial fishing and lobstering. In other words, this is a working harbor. The dock and the buildings on its shores are part of the lobstermen's cooperative. Smells of salt water and lobster bait permeate the air. Traps and buoys piled on the dock signal that this community makes its living from the sea.

William Otis Sawtelle, a professor at Haverford College in Pennsylvania, summered on Little Cranberry in the early part of the last century. His interest in island life led him to amass a sizable collection of documents and artifacts related to this region. Sawtelle founded the Islesford Histori-cal Society, and in 1919 he purchased a shorefront building that had been a ship's chandlery. The "Blue Duck," as Sawtelle named it, served to store and exhibit the society's collection.

By 1927 the material gathered by Sawtelle had exceeded the capacity of the Blue Duck, so he commissioned the brick structure that continues today as the Islesford Historical Museum. Do-

The brick building that houses the museum was commissioned in 1927.

William Otis Sawtelle founded the Islesford Historical Museum.

nated to Acadia National Park in 1948, it houses an extensive collection of artifacts relating to island life; documents and charts from the region's early explorers; shipboards and scrolls from old sailing vessels; and tools, furnishings, and photographs of early island dwellers. All these combine to tell the rich and colorful story of the Cranberry Isles.

Sawtelle's lantern is on display.

Museum exhibits portray the lives of the early island settlers.

The Elisha Gilley house is one of only a few buildings left to represent what was once a thriving community.

Baker Island

Of the five islands in the Cranberry archipelago, Baker is the most isolated, although at very low tides a bar nearly connects it to Little Cranberry. In the summer, daily boat tours leave from Northeast Harbor, but landing on the island is always dependent on the wind and the surf.

Six miles from Northeast Harbor, Baker Island is nearly round and measures about a half-mile in diameter. At its highest point—ninety-two feet above sea level, in the center of the island—sits a lighthouse. Built in 1828, the light still guides vessels into and out of Frenchman Bay, and it serves as a point of reference for all the boats operating in the area. In 1855 the keeper's house was built, and the tower was sheathed in brick to reinforce its wooden frame. The light was automated in 1966 and is now solar powered. Although the surrounding land is part of Acadia, the lighthouse continues to be maintained by the U.S. Coast Guard.

Today, most of Baker Island is heavily forested, but early photographs show a cleared, open landscape. "Main Street," the well-worn path leading

Baker's lighthouse is positioned at the center of the island.

from the boat landing to the lighthouse, reveals signs of a once-thriving community: a well that still holds fresh water, a one-room schoolhouse (now converted to a summer cottage), old foundations overgrown with vegetation, and a graveyard that chronicles the lives of the families that once called this island home.

The people who settled here were pioneers, in the true sense of the word. Isolated from the mainland, they drew their livelihoods from the sea and from whatever resources this small island could provide. For 123 years, the Gilleys and other families lived and worked on Baker Island. The population fluctuated over the years: The 1850 census records thirty-four residents, but descendants of the Gilleys claim that at one time there were as many as sixty-five individuals in the community.

As land transportation developed and towns on the mainland grew in size, so did employment opportunities there. The children of island families along the Maine coast were drawn to this more promising lifestyle, and many never returned. The isolated communities slowly dwindled and died. Baker was one such island. Its last permanent resident, Albert Stanley, moved away in 1929, and the lighthouse keeper left in 1966. With the passing of this era, the island has returned to its natural state. The vegetation has grown back, and many of the houses have been reduced to mere foundations. Except for a few standing buildings, the graveyard, and a small plot of land on the south beach, the entire island is now part of Acadia. The park service maintains the white house that was built by Elisha Gilley in the 1840s and periodically mows the meadow in order to preserve what many consider to be the most spectacular view of Mount Desert Island.

Beyond Main Street and the lighthouse is an island habitat that reaches into the cold Atlantic and whose plants have adapted to this nearly subarctic environment. The silverweed cinquefoil *(Potentilla anserina)*; sea lungwort, or oysterleaf *(Mertensia maritima)*; and the (arctic) beach iris

Baker provides a stunning view of Acadia's glacier-sculpted mountains.

can all be found on the Baker's granite coastline.

Crossing the island to the south beach reveals a very different scene. Large sheets of granite, carved by the surf, have been piled into a giant, angular seawall. The gentle waves of a warm summer day give little indication of how this shoreline was created. But the positioning of the big granite slabs speaks volumes about the power that winter storms, raging through the Gulf of Maine, unleash upon this exposed shoreline.

Those who are fortunate enough to spend even an afternoon on Baker will experience the wildness and isolation that typify Maine islands and will gain some appreciation of what life was like for the hardy individuals who settled them.

Silverweed cinquefoil (Potentilla anserina)

Schoodic Peninsula

Part of the mainland, this peninsula forms the eastern shore of Frenchman Bay. It is forty-five miles (about an hour's drive) from Bar Harbor. Follow Route 3 off Mount Desert Island to Ellsworth, then take Route 1 to West Gouldsboro and Route 186 to Winter Harbor. Turn right in Winter Harbor, and follow the signs to Schoodic Point and Acadia National Park.

The name Schoodic most likely comes from the Micmac word *eskevodek,* meaning "the end," or the Passamaquoddy word *scoudiac,* meaning "great clear place," which may have been given after a fire leveled the landscape.

Like those of any landmass in contact with the sea, the peninsula's climate and shoreline are dominated by the wind, the currents, and the surf. From dramatic cliffs to exposed headlands and gentle cobble beaches, Schoodic is a microcosm of Maine's varied shorelines. The seven-mile, one-way road provides an opportunity to explore these different habitats. At several points along the western shore, short trails lead down to the ocean, where sheer cliffs drop to the water's edge. From this vantage point there are views across the bay to the eastern peaks of Mount Desert Island.

Approximately two miles from the park entrance, a dirt road on the left winds nearly to the 440-foot summit of Schoodic Head, the highest point on the peninsula. Although not completely open, the summit provides interesting views to the east and west. This section of the peninsula has one of Maine's largest and densest stands of jack pine, a tree that is at the southern edge of its range here. Paired, blunt needles and a gnarled appearance are key to its identification. Rarely growing to more than sixty feet in height, the jack pine succeeds on its ability to out-compete its rivals. Requiring open sunlight, the trees do well in areas that have previously been cut over or burned. Its cones have adapted to fire and may remain sealed for years until flames heat the resin that seals them shut, causing the cones to open and disperse their seeds. In the ashy soil of a freshly burned forest, the jack pine seeds get a head start in colonizing the newly vacated real estate.

At the foot of Schoodic Head, take a left and continue on the one-way paved road, bearing right toward Schoodic Point. The drama of the sea erupting on this granite headland is captivating. The great granite steps that march into the ocean create a playground for the surf at nearly every tide.

The bedrock at Schoodic Point tells the geologic story of the area's dramatic creation. The

Schoodic's western shore has dramatic cliff faces.

granite was formed by a rising mass of molten rock that was halted in its upward movement several miles beneath the surface, where it slowly cooled to stone. The eventual release of pressure caused the granite to crack in many directions. In time, black basaltic lava oozed into these cracks, producing dramatic markings known as dikes. Four hundred million years of weathering, several million years of glacial action, and continual erosion by the sea have exposed this event, now frozen in time on the peninsula's rocky shore. Although such dikes are found in many places in the park, Schoodic's are some of the largest and most complex in the region.

The surf erupts dramatically on the granite headland of Schoodic Peninsula.

Schoodic's basaltic dikes are truly impressive.

The herring gulls are always looking for an easy meal.

The herring gulls in this area are particularly numerous and can be bothersome. Because Schoodic is a great place for a picnic on a warm summer day, these birds have learned that, for the price of a photograph, they can get a free meal. Once fed, they lose their natural fear of humans and soon become persistent beggars. All gulls should be considered wild animals that are potentially dangerous when approached too closely. At Schoodic, they provide a much-needed service, scavenging the shoreline for any bit of decaying matter. They can also be seen hunting for sea urchins and sea stars in the shallows at low tide. The herring gulls are more than capable of supporting themselves without human interference.

Just offshore from Schoodic Point is a thirty-acre island known as Little Moose. This fragile environment is home to a number of arctic-alpine plant species, such as pearlwort, blinks, birdseye primrose, and oysterleaf. The island features a small bog, a salt marsh, and a shoreline that varies from cobble beaches to dramatic cliffs. Hiking to Little Moose Island is possible at low tide, when a sandbar connects it to the mainland. If you decide to visit this special place, stay on the trails and leave the flora and fauna undisturbed for others to enjoy.

From Schoodic Point, the one-way road continues along the eastern shore of the peninsula. The dense spruce forest on the left is contrasted by a series of cobble-filled coves on the right. In several locations, small parking areas allow you to pull off and climb down to explore this quiet shoreline.

The story of how Schoodic Peninsula became part of Acadia reads like a suspense novel, complete with unfulfilled dreams and political intrigue. In the late 1890s John G. Moore purchased the land with the intent to preserve it as a park. A native of coastal Maine, he had moved to New York as a young man and made his fortune. Upon Moore's return to his home state he began working toward his longtime goal of developing this section of the coast, just as Bar Harbor had been developed on Mount Desert Island. His plans had yet to be carried out when he died in 1898.

Thirty years later his second wife and two daughters fulfilled his dream for Schoodic by offering the land to George Dorr and the national park. However, the 1919 Congressional act that had elevated Acadia from a national monument to a national park (Sieur de Monts National Monument became Lafayette National Park) stipulated that the park could acquire land only by donation and mandated that the property had to be on Mount Desert Island. Dorr and his political connections quickly proposed a bill that would expand the park's charter to allow the acquisition of land beyond MDI.

Another problem associated with this donation was the park's name—Lafayette. Being good English ladies, the daughters of John Moore felt the name was inappropriate. Dorr responded, "The name of Lafayette was taken because of the strong wartime feeling at the time of the park's creation; I have often since thought that Acadia, because of its old historical association and descriptive character, would have been far better." In 1929 Congress passed a bill that allowed the acquisition of Schoodic Peninsula and simultaneously changed the park's name to Acadia.

Little Moose Island has a fascinating arctic-alpine plant community.

Schoodic's eastern shore is a series of cobble beaches.

Isle au Haut

The influx of summer tourists to the coast of Maine in the 1850s began the inexorable transformation of small fishing villages into trendy resorts. Those looking for a quiet coastal village, where Nature and the sea dominate daily life, will no longer find it in towns such as Camden, Boothbay, or Bar Harbor. Fortunately, working harbors and undeveloped real estate still exist in a few out-of-the-way locations along the coast. Isle au Haut is such a place.

In the past, it, too, experienced periods of growth and development, but life on this island today more closely reflects a Maine coastal village of the early 1800s. A two-hour drive from Bar Harbor to Stonington, plus an hour's boat ride delivers you to the town landing. (The boat then continues to Duck Harbor on the far side of the island, in Acadia National Park.) The number of visitors to Isle au Haut is limited by the scarcity of campsites at Duck Harbor and by the available seating on the mail boat. (Day-trippers must watch the time in order to catch the afternoon run back to Stonington.)

A gravel road circles the island, but few residents use the entire circuit because much of it is narrow and nearly impassable. Your exploration of Isle au Haut should begin at Duck Harbor, where you can follow either the Western Head Trail or the Goat Trail.

The paths along the southern shoreline intermittently wind from open ocean vistas to dark evergreen woodlands and from intimate harbors lined with pebble beaches to dramatic rocky headlands. Hiking may be strenuous at times, but your efforts will be well rewarded. Where the trails emerge from the forest onto the exposed headlands, the unusual rock formations at your feet will undoubtedly catch your attention. The island's geology is a complex mixture of granite and volcanic rocks shaped by the surf and by the glacial ice that at one time stretched into the Gulf of Maine.

During his 1604 exploration of Penobscot Bay, Samuel de Champlain named this place "Isle Haute," meaning high island. Mount Desert Island and Isle au Haut were both important to sailors of the day because their mountains could be seen from far out to sea and thus were useful as navigational references. Six miles long and two-and-one-half miles wide, Isle au Haut stands out among the smaller, lower islands nearby. It is, indeed, high, featuring a small but distinctive range of mountains, the tallest of which is 440-foot Mount Champlain.

Today, island communities may seem isolated,

The town landing sits at the edge of Isle au Haut's thorofare.

A rough but scenic road circles the island.

but to the early settlers, who made their living from the sea, being five or ten miles closer to their fishing grounds was a distinct advantage. Long before roads and carriages, schooners and sloops were the primary modes of transportation along the Maine coast, so living on an island was hardly a disadvantage. As early as the 1820s Isle au Haut had a healthy fishing fleet, and by the mid-1870s, its population was about 350. Early American settlers were not the first to realize the convenience of island living. Shell heaps throughout Isle au Haut mark the location of Native American encampments and tell of the bountiful food and productive lifestyle of these first residents.

In the late 1870s Ernest W. Bowditch first saw

The summit of Duck Harbor Mountain overlooks the island's western shore.

Isle au Haut's hiking trails traverse densely wooded paths...

Isle au Haut from the deck of a steamer. Intrigued, he purchased land and with some friends established the Isle au Haut Company. These men bought the existing Chowder House and converted it to the Point Lookout Club, a private fishing club. The group's interest in the island and the local residents led to its funding a number of improvements, including a school, town hall, and library, as well as a road that connected to Western Head on the far side of the island. In 1942 the children of Ernest Bowditch—Richard, Sarah, and Elizabeth—donated a large portion of the company's land holdings to Acadia National Park. In his letter to Harold Ickes, the then secretary of the

…exposed rocky outcrops…

…and small intimate harbors.

The island has a healthy population of white-tailed deer.

interior, Richard Bowditch describes the gift as "a wild land very largely covered for the most part with spruce, pine, birch, and woods containing several good harbors for small boats. The property also contains a freshwater lake a mile-and-a-half in length. There are numerous hills and trails and some roadway. . . We believe that the people of the country will be benefited by having this property added to the national park area."

As with all the land in Acadia, the twenty-eight hundred-plus acres on Isle au Haut were given for the purpose of preserving a piece of Maine's natural beauty. Today, as a result, much of the island is as it was before human habitation.

The sun clears the horizon beyond Seawall.

After exploring Acadia's Loop Road and the less accessible areas covered in this book, you will have undoubtedly discovered that the park's beauty lies not only in its unique landscape or its rich natural and human history, but also in its nearly limitless diversity. From open mountaintops and rugged shorelines to densely wooded paths and delicate plant communities, the park succeeds in preserving the best of Maine's coastal environment. Acadia does not pretend to be a wilderness park, but rather serves as a passageway from the chaos of urban life into the tranquillity of the natural world. Going beyond the Park Loop Road is the first step, but there is still more.

To find the true soul of Nature, one must leave the paved road entirely and strike out on foot along the trails and carriage roads that lead into the heart of Acadia National Park.

We intend to lead you on this remarkable journey with the next book in our Acadia series.

The moon rises over Great Cranberry Island.

References

The following sources were used to confirm dates and facts, and they are recommended for further information concerning the topics covered in this book.

Chapman, Carleton A., *The Geology of Acadia National Park* (The Chatham Press, Inc., 1970)

Coffin, Tammis, *Description of sites in Acadia National Park selected for evaluation as national natural landmarks by the critical areas program* (Acadia National Park 1990)

Collier, Sargent F., *Mount Desert Island & Acadia National Park: An Informal History* (Down East Books, Camden, ME, 1978)

Dorr, George B., *The Story of Acadia National Park*, (Acadia Publishing Co., Bar Harbor, ME, 1997)

Eastman, John, *Forest and Thicket: Trees, Shrubs and Wildflowers of Eastern North America* (Stackpole Books, Harrisburg, PA, 1992)

Elfring, Chris, *AMC Guide to Mount Desert and Acadia National Park* (Appalachian Mountain Club Books, Boston, MA, 1993)

Fernald Meg, *One Man's Museum—The story of the Islesford Historical Museum* (Eastern National Park & Monument Association, 1990)

Gilman, Richard A., *The Geology of Mount Desert Island.* (Maine Geological Survey Department of Conservation, 1986)

Gosner, Kenneth L., *A Field Guide to the Atlantic Seashore.* The Peterson Field Guide Series. (Houghton Mifflin Co., Boston, 1978)

Haines, Arther and Thomas F.Vining, *Flora of Maine: a Manual for Identification of Native and Naturalized Vascular Plants of Maine.* (V.F. Thomas Co., Bar Harbor, ME, 1998)

Hansen, Gunnar; Editor, *Mount Desert, An Informal History.* (Published by the Town of Mount Desert, 1989)

Mancinelli, Isabel, *Baker Island Cultural Landscape Report.* (National Park Service files, 1996)

Mazlish, Anne, Editor, *The Tracy Log Book 1855, A Month in Summer.* (Acadia Publishing Co., 1997)

McLane, Charles B., *Islands of the Mid-Maine Coast, Penobscot and Blue Hill Bays.* Volume I. (Kennebec River Press, Inc., Falmouth, ME, 1982)

McLane, Charles B. *Islands of the Mid-Maine Coast, Mount Desert to Machias Bay.* Volume II. (Kennebec River Press, Inc., Falmouth, ME, 1989)

Morrison, Samuel Eliot, *The Story of Mount Desert Island* (Little Brown and Company, Boston, MA, 1960)

Peattie, Donald, *The Natural History of Trees of Eastern and Central North America,* (Houghton Mifflin Co., Boston MA, 1991)

Raup Henry A., *Four Generations in Maine—The Carroll Homestead Southwest Harbor 1825–1917,* (Eastern National Park and Monuments Association, 1993)

Rieley, William D. and Roxanne S.Brouse, *Historic Resource Study for the Carriage Road System, Acadia National Park* (Rieley & Associates, Charlottesville, VA 1989)

Rothe, Robert, *ACADIA, the Story Behind the Scenery* (KC Publications, Las Vegas NV, 1979)

Spurling, Ted, *The Town of Cranberry Isles—A Thumbnail Sketch of Five Maine Islands* (Van Houten Graphics, Brownsville, VT, 1986)

More good reading from Down East Books

If you enjoyed *Beyond the Park Loop Road,* **you'll want to know about these other Down East titles:**

The Park Loop Road, by Robert Thayer. Acadia's twenty-one-mile-long Loop Road was designed in the 1930s by noted landscape architect Frederick Law Olmstead Jr. to "lead one through a series of visual experiences." This book guides the visitor through the unparalleled scenic beauty, dramatic geology, and historic importance of this extraordinary road. 0-89272-443-9

Lost Bar Harbor, by G. W. Helfrich and Gladys O'Neil. The summer "cottages" of Mount Desert Island set a standard for luxury in the late nineteenth and early twentieth centuries. Here are eighty-six of the splendid structures that once graced the town of Bar Harbor. Some were lost to greed, some to pragmatism, and many to the great fire of 1947. Their like will not be seen again. 0-89272-142-1

Discovering Old Bar Harbor and Acadia National Park: An Unconventional History and Guide, by Ruth Ann Hill. The township of Bar Harbor encompasses more than a third of Mount Desert Island, including the most visited parts of Acadia National Park. Searching for Bar Harbor's past is a bit of a treasure hunt, but many things become evident once one knows where to look. This unusual guidebook tells just where to find traces of Bar Harbor's fascinating history. 0-89272-355-6

Mount Desert Island and Acadia National Park: An Informal History, photographs and text by Sargent F. Collier. The best from three classics about Bar Harbor, Mount Desert Island, and Acadia National Park. Edited by G. W. Helfrich. Heavily illustrated with the author, Sargent Collier's photographs of the contemporary scene and earlier prints of the good old days. 0-89272-044-1

Mr. Rockefeller's Roads: The Untold Story of Acadia's Carriage Roads & Their Creator, Ann Rockefeller Roberts. Acadia's fifty-one miles of carriage roads are the result of decades of personal effort by philanthropist John D. Rockefeller Jr. Here, JDR Jr.'s granddaughter recounts the fascinating story of Acadia's "Rockefeller Roads" and of a man ahead of his time. 0-89272-296-7

Acadia National Park: Maine's Intimate Parkland, photographs and text by Alan Nyiri. From its impressive vistas to its tiniest treasures, Acadia is an island parkland of haunting beauty. This magnificent collection of color photographs captures that beauty. 0-89272-219-3

The Mount Desert Island Pocket Guide Series
A Pocket Guide to Biking on Mt. Desert Island, by Audrey Shelton Minutolo. 0-89272-367-X
A Pocket Guide to Paddling the Waters of Mt. Desert Island, by Earl Brechlin. 0-89272-357-2
A Pocket Guide to Hiking on Mt. Desert Island, by Earl Brechlin. 0-89272-356-4
A Pocket Guide to the Carriage Roads of Acadia National Park, 2nd Edition, by Diana F. Abrell. 0-89272-349-1

Check your local bookstore, or order from Down East Books at 800-685-7962
Visa and MasterCard Accepted